# SPEED ZONE
# SUPERFAST BOATS

by Alicia Z. Klepeis

pogo

# Ideas for Parents and Teachers

Pogo Books let children practice reading informational text while introducing them to nonfiction features such as headings, labels, sidebars, maps, and diagrams, as well as a table of contents, glossary, and index.

Carefully leveled text with a strong photo match offers early fluent readers the support they need to succeed.

## Before Reading

- "Walk" through the book and point out the various nonfiction features. Ask the student what purpose each feature serves.
- Look at the glossary together. Read and discuss the words.

## Read the Book

- Have the child read the book independently.
- Invite him or her to list questions that arise from reading.

## After Reading

- Discuss the child's questions. Talk about how he or she might find answers to those questions.
- Prompt the child to think more. Ask: How do speedboats go so fast? Can you think of any other superfast vehicles?

Pogo Books are published by Jump!
5357 Penn Avenue South
Minneapolis, MN 55419
www.jumplibrary.com

Library of Congress Cataloging-in-Publication Data

Names: Klepeis, Alicia, 1971- author.
Title: Superfast boats / by Alicia Z. Klepeis.
Description: Minneapolis, MN: Jump!, Inc., [2022]
Series: Speed zone
Includes index. | Audience: Ages 7-10
Identifiers: LCCN 2020047830 (print)
LCCN 2020047831 (ebook)
ISBN 9781645279556 (hardcover)
ISBN 9781645279563 (paperback)
ISBN 9781645279570 (ebook)
Subjects: LCSH: Motorboats–Design and construction–Juvenile literature.
Motorboats–Speed–Juvenile literature.
Classification: LCC VM341 .K54 2022 (print)
LCC VM341 (ebook) | DDC 623.82/31–dc23
LC record available at https://lccn.loc.gov/2020047830
LC ebook record available at https://lccn.loc.gov/2020047831

Editor: Eliza Leahy
Designer: Molly Ballanger

Photo Credits: Darren Brode/Shutterstock, cover, 4, 12-13; Gertan/Shutterstock, 1; Batareykin/Dreamstime, 3; Jesse Cobb Photography/iStock, 5; muratart/Shutterstock, 6-7, 23; Felipe Oliveira/Dreamstime, 8-9; freevideophotoagency/Shutterstock, 10; Imagesupply/Dreamstime, 11; Nielskliim/Shutterstock, 14-15; William Hoover Iiii/Dreamstime, 16; joan Ilado/Alamy, 17; Martin Barraud/Getty, 18-19; Mauro Rodrigues/Shutterstock, 20-21.

Printed in the United States of America at Corporate Graphics in North Mankato, Minnesota.

# TABLE OF CONTENTS

**CHAPTER 1**
**Powerful Engines** . . . . . . . . . . . . . . . . . . . . . . . . 4

**CHAPTER 2**
**Hull Design** . . . . . . . . . . . . . . . . . . . . . . . . . . . . . 10

**CHAPTER 3**
**Speedy Boats** . . . . . . . . . . . . . . . . . . . . . . . . . . . . 16

**ACTIVITIES & TOOLS**
**Try This!** . . . . . . . . . . . . . . . . . . . . . . . . . . . . . . . . 22
**Glossary** . . . . . . . . . . . . . . . . . . . . . . . . . . . . . . . . 23
**Index** . . . . . . . . . . . . . . . . . . . . . . . . . . . . . . . . . . 24
**To Learn More** . . . . . . . . . . . . . . . . . . . . . . . . . . . 24

# CHAPTER 1

# POWERFUL ENGINES

Whoosh! A boat skips across the waves. Water sprays behind it. It is a speedboat! These boats can go more than 100 miles (161 kilometers) per hour!

Boats float because of an upward **force** called **buoyancy**. When a boat is placed in water, it pushes water out of its way. If a boat weighs more than the water it **displaces**, it sinks. If it weighs less, it floats.

**engine**

It takes a lot of force
for a boat to move fast.
This force is measured
in **horsepower** (HP).
HP comes from **engines**.
Faster boats need more HP.

Engines power **propellers**.
Propellers turn in the water.
They push boats forward.
Larger boats often have
several engines. Why?
This gives them more power.

◀ · · · · · **propeller**

# TAKE A LOOK!

What are the parts of a speedboat? Take a look!

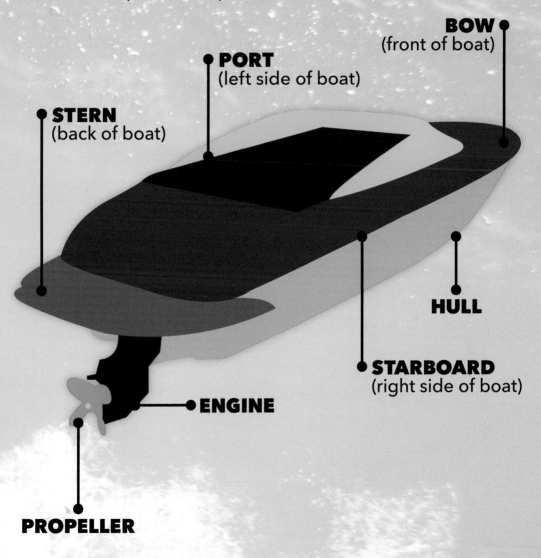

**BOW**
(front of boat)

**PORT**
(left side of boat)

**STERN**
(back of boat)

**HULL**

**STARBOARD**
(right side of boat)

**ENGINE**

**PROPELLER**

# CHAPTER 2

# HULL DESIGN

What else affects a boat's speed? One factor is size. Bigger boats are usually heavier. They need more power to move fast. Smaller boats don't need as much HP.

**V-shaped hull**

Hull design also affects speed. V-shaped hulls are most common for speedboats. These hulls **skim** the water's surface. This creates less **friction** between the boat and the water. It allows for more speed.

hydroplane

GRAHA
TRUCKING, IN

7

A hydroplane boat is light and fast. Only a small part of its hull touches the water when traveling fast. The boat is designed to trap air underneath it. This air lifts the boat as it moves forward.

Hulls are often hollow inside. The lighter weight allows boats to move fast.

Some boats have two hulls. With two hulls, less of the boat's bottom touches the water. This creates less water **resistance**. These boats are called catamarans.

## DID YOU KNOW?

Hulls on fast boats are made of strong but light materials, such as **carbon fiber**.

catamaran

hull

hull

# CHAPTER 3

# SPEEDY BOATS

There are many types of speedboats. Drag boats are some of the fastest. Drag boat races can be just 1,000 feet (305 meters) long. These boats can finish in under four seconds!

drag boat

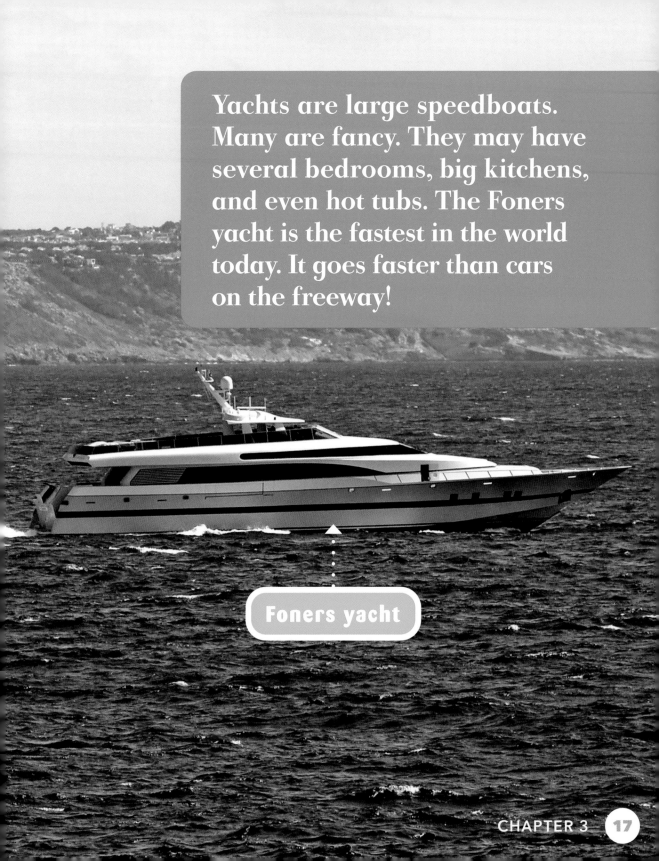

Yachts are large speedboats. Many are fancy. They may have several bedrooms, big kitchens, and even hot tubs. The Foners yacht is the fastest in the world today. It goes faster than cars on the freeway!

Foners yacht

A jet boat's engine connects to a jet. The jet takes in water. Then it shoots water out of a **nozzle** at the back of the boat. This pushes the boat forward. With no propellers, jet boats skim the surface of the water. They can travel in water less than two inches (5.1 centimeters) deep!

## DID YOU KNOW?

The Bluebird K7 is a jet boat. In 1964, it went 276 miles (444 km) per hour! This makes it the second-fastest boat ever.

Bluebird K7

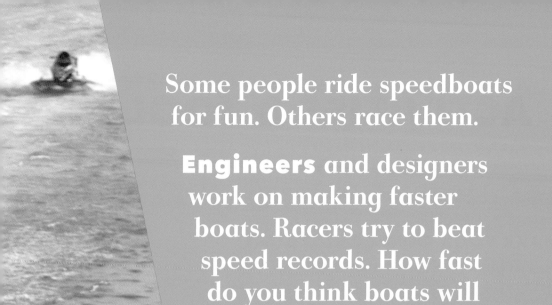

Some people ride speedboats for fun. Others race them.

**Engineers** and designers work on making faster boats. Racers try to beat speed records. How fast do you think boats will go in the future?

## DID YOU KNOW?

Boat designers are working on **efficient** fast boats. Some run on **solar power** or other green energy sources. That's a win!

# ACTIVITIES & TOOLS

## MAKE YOUR OWN CARGO BOAT

**Design your own cargo boat and test how much weight it can hold.**

**What You Need:**
- paper
- pencil
- aluminum foil
- sink or basin of water
- pennies, beans, or other small objects

1. **Sketch some simple boat designs that you think would be able to carry weight without sinking. How many hulls will each design have?**

2. **Construct a boat using aluminum foil. You can add layers to make it stronger.**

3. **Place the boat in a sink or basin filled with water. Add pennies or other weights one at a time. How many can your boat hold before it sinks?**

4. **Using a different design, construct a second boat with the aluminum foil.**

5. **Repeat Step 3. Which boat held more weight? Why do you think that was?**

# GLOSSARY

**buoyancy:** The upward force that causes a boat to float when in water.

**carbon fiber:** A strong, lightweight material that is made up of mainly carbon atoms and is used to make vehicle parts.

**displaces:** Moves something from its usual place.

**efficient:** Uses less energy to perform a task.

**engineers:** People who are specially trained to design and build machines or large structures.

**engines:** Machines that make things move by using gasoline, steam, or another energy source.

**force:** Any action that produces, stops, or changes the shape or movement of an object.

**friction:** The force that slows down objects when they rub against each other.

**horsepower:** A unit for measuring the power of an engine.

**hull:** The body or frame of a boat or ship.

**nozzle:** A short tube on a hose or pipe that controls the flow of liquid, gas, or air.

**propellers:** Sets of rotating blades that provide force to move an object through air or water.

**resistance:** The force that works against the motion of an object.

**skim:** To glide across or pass quickly and lightly over something.

**solar power:** Energy from the sun that can be used for heating and generating electricity.

# INDEX

Bluebird K7 18

buoyancy 5

carbon fiber 14

catamarans 14

displaces 5

drag boats 16

engineers 21

engines 7, 8, 9, 18

Foners yacht 17

force 5, 7

friction 11

horsepower (HP) 7, 10

hull 9, 11, 13, 14

hydroplane boat 13

jet boat 18

materials 14

nozzle 18

propellers 8, 9, 18

races 16, 21

resistance 14

sinks 5

size 10

weighs 5

yachts 17

# TO LEARN MORE

Finding more information is as easy as 1, 2, 3.

❶ Go to www.factsurfer.com

❷ Enter "superfastboats" into the search box.

❸ Choose your book to see a list of websites.

**FACT
SURFER**